AMERICA! WHAT'S MY NAME?

America!
What's My Name?

The "Other" Poets Unfurl the Flag

Frank X Walker, Editor

WIND PUBLICATIONS

America! What's My Name? Copyright © 2007 by Frank X Walker. All rights reserved. Printed in the United States of America. No part of this book may be reproduced without permission, except in the case of brief quotations embodied in critical articles or reviews. For information address Wind Publications, 600 Overbrook Drive, Nicholasville KY 40356.

First edition

International Standard Book Number   978-1-893239-63-0
Library of Congress Control Number   2007931233

Front cover design by Bryant Wells.

Thanks to the editors of the following journals where these poems first appeared:

The Drunken Boat — "The Price of Lamb"
The Louisville Review — "13 Ways of Looking at a Black Man"

Contents

Kathy Y. Wilson   1
    "will [my] America know me when i land

Suheir Hammad   5
    On Refuge and Language
    Fasting Food
    Black Silver

Kelly Norman Ellis   12
    The Letting Down of Milk

Christine Rose James   14
    Jackfruit Leaves
    Bandit Memory

Frank X Walker   16
    Black Buddha
    The Price of Lamb
    Thirteen Ways of Looking at a Blackman

Ellen Hagan   21
    conjwoman
    Poem # 1 / break me
    Plan B

Tiffany Midge   24
    What is the Sound of America
    Her Kind of Horses
    Matrimonial Vows for Cannibals

Yael Flusberg   29
   Columbia Road Passover
   Sukkot
   Tu Beshvat
   Back to the Beginning
   Los Bolos
   Making Love Transparent

Parneshia Jones   40
   100 Storms of Slaughter
   Georgia on My Mind
   Sacrifice

Patricia Smith   46
   Heck
   Looting
   What Was the First Sound
   Character Study

Roger Bonair-Agard   50
   Brisbane, 1975
   To Mimic Magic
   Soul

Hao Wang   62
   The News
   Sight
   Lessons
   Meditations on a Restaurant Hamburger
   Today

Bianca Spriggs — 71
  Salt Skin
  Except Thou Bless Me
  Surface Tension
  Couples Skate
  Chow Time

Matthew Shenoda — 83
  Voices from the Rubble
  Reality

Maria Blackhorse — 85
  Mother Love
  Power Song

Anne Shelby — 88
  Kentucky Junction

Mitchell L.H. Douglas — 90
  Another Season
  Plastic
  Lineage

Debra Kang Dean — 96
  "Of Thee I Sing"
  Punchbowl

Adrian Matejka — 101
  Cannibalism
  "Carefree as a Plantation Darky in Watermelon Time"
  White Women: Lola Toy

Lee Newton 107
    Invitation
    Everything Broken
    The Unbroken
    A Language Lost
    Why We Make Love
    Sabotage
    Egrets on the Pond
    Some Men Do

Luis Urrea 116
    There Is a Town in Mexico
    Walking Backward in the Dark

Contributors' biographies 123

Introduction

The degree to which university professors have staked their academic lives and intellectual selves on every accented syllable of dead white men, having diagramed their "brilliant" intentions and held it up as evidence that poetry is the caviar on the literary menu, has helped carve out an elitist mystique and ruined many a promising young poet. In the pages that follow, we offer a counter argument: that poetry is bread. That it is whole grain sustenance and comes in all colors, ethnicities, sizes, genders, and sexual preferences. It is not just the leather-bound private joy of scholars, but new and naked and pouring out of the stomachs and hearts of emerging and established writers all over this country.

America needs poetry more than it needs prisons; ill-conceived government policies, inadequate schools, political spin, or exit polls. Poetry, when used correctly, is the most democratic thing we own. It belongs to the people. It is for the people and it rings truest when written by the people.

You probably won't find these poets in your syllabus, though there are more prize-winning writers in these pages than you will find in many university English departments. But wherever you can find a table or a hungry mouth; wherever people need nothing else with their soup but homemade biscuits, cornbread, tortillas, challah, or frybread, fresh out of the oven, I hope you will find this book being read aloud or passed hand to hand with love, with appreciation for genuine solutions for real hunger.

America is hungry for truth and it's being served right here, right now.

— Frank X Walker, December 2006

America! What's My Name?

The "Other" Poets Unfurl the Flag

Kathy Y. Wilson

"will [my] America know me when i land?"

written before jumping from a 2nd-story window

i know from identity crisis
in the throes of one right now
the fissures in my professional emotional spiritual
mental physical and even racial selves converged to
form one large fault line along which my own private
idaho is lined up to fall the fuck inside
deep inside i'm sayin
you feel me/you are me
living in miss America as we know is not all cosby
condi and powell
and the black and white of all of that is downright
embarrassing because what about the yellows the reds
the browns and the mongrels the towel heads and dot
heads/the alphabet-soup named ones and their funny
gods
we're all searching
wanna be respected be seen be validated be counted
not in some census shit
wanna be counted as in: in, gotdammit
but America that bitch depends on us to be lost and
self-loathing/she wants us turning our pockets inside
out looking for id cards
if we do not know fundamentally whom we are then we
won't know what not to let America call us
who is she to be pontificating on identity while her
own flops about in crisis
i am you that's who i am/i told you i am/you
i believe in nothing
nothing but the blood of jesus and the possibilities

of deliverance/deliverance from the evil of being
ignored and overlooked blamed and set aside
misunderstood laughed at and underestimated
this is what America does to us the Other
i don't know about you but She has called me out of
my name so many times it's like i look around every
time i hear/i almost answer to sapphire mammy black
bitch mule of de world dyke freak misanthrope bigot
auntie weirdo loner manic depressive lip biter eyelash
puller obsessive compulsive weed head wannabe fraud
liar brilliant under/educated unmotivated sinner
abomination grief stricken loudmouthed diabetic
overweight overwrought undone outdone lost frustrated
angry dyslexic broke ass smart alec
and because i bought fully into the gimmickry of the
distraction of the preoccupation with race America
pricks up my (r)ear when she start talkin that ole
African nigger colored nigger nigga niggra afro
American/black/african American nigga/nigger hamilton
American/black/black American/American shit
living in a postmodern/post-9/11 America is like
being a lifelong losing contestant in the myth America
contest
it is maddening
when we buy into it is when we're really lost/losing
our minds trying to fit perfectly into a paradigm that
will never be cast in our collective likeness
the Others get it but them others don't and that is
that America will crush us unless we rise up and
wrestle her to the ground/grunting wheezing sweating
demanding that She call off Her dogs with all that
hatred shit/all that inhumanity/all that killing us
softly with Her wrong
America likes Her some underdogs/some niggers though
if the Others were honest we'd confess we're all
trying to get away from the nigger in us once it's

lost its hip shelf life
it's like the great American poet paul mooney
says/everybody wanna be a nigga/don't nobody wanna be
a nigga
and isn't that what America is saying to all the
Others among us
that we're lowly/we're niggers
arguably the most vile or at least as randall kennedy
says/troublesome/word we have
latinos aka hispanics dba wetbacks are perennially
the new niggers   but every ethnic category
imagined by the census bureau has its population of
niggers
i mean the classism/the shit's funny after awhile
i haven't laughed so hard at some nigger shit since
michael richards did penance for saying 50 years ago
we'd have had you hanging upside down from a tree with
a fork up yer ass by going on jesse jackson's radio
show to the strains of marvin's what's goin
on/yeah/i'll tell you what's goin on
laughter's the only thing left once we reconcile the
ideal and idyllic Americas/the twins trump everything
and everyone especially the motherfuckers clawing to
comprise them/to live like them
i need America, What's My Name as desperately as the
next motherfuckin Other/tying off a vein hope it ain't
in vein/takin another hit hope it'll hit/like stevie
said where were you when i needed you like right now
shhhh/mama's here now
if you're in this choir this book preaches to then
pass it along because nearly every other tactic has
failed/take it back to the old school word of mouth
somebody do this work please
don't know about you but now i am tired
i am disappointed
America said integrate/so we moved

America said vote/so we punched chads
America said get a degree/so we agreed
America said come/so we swam
then when we dissent America forgets she was founded
on tea parties underground railroads last stands
internment camps and beat generations/generations have
assembled in a cluster-fuck collection of/yes/poems as
identity cards/as fingerprints/as dna in unrhymed
verse
no longer relying/as much as my black my closeted
liberal my outré dyke self wants/on do-nothing
democrats and fair-weather well-meaning whites to do
anything lasting about this segregationist fear factor
we function with in America/ima be a new wave
revolutionary/ima read these poems aloud:
to America:
now turn over
face down in the pillow
ass up
what's my name
say it
say my name/my/name/my
say/it
my name

Suheir Hammad

On Refuge and Language

I do not wish
To place words in living mouths
Or bury the dead dishonorably

I am not deaf to cries escaping shelters
That citizens are not refugees
Refugees are not Americans

I will not use language
One way or another
To accommodate my comfort

I will not look away

All I know is this

No peoples ever choose to claim status of dispossessed
No peoples want pity above compassion
No enslaved peoples ever called themselves slaves

What do we pledge allegiance to?

A government that leaves its old
To die of thirst surrounded by water
Is a foreign government

People who are streaming
Illiterate into paperwork
Have long ago been abandoned

I think of coded language

And all that words carry on their backs

I think of how it is always the poor
Who are tagged and boxed with labels
Not of their own choosing

I think of my grandparents
And how some called them refugees
Others called them non-existent
They called themselves landless
Which means homeless

Before the hurricane
No tents were prepared for the fleeing
Because Americans do not live in tents
Tents are for Haiti for Bosnia for Rwanda

Refugees are the rest of the world

Those left to defend their human decency
Against conditions the rich keep their animals from
Those who have too many children
Those who always have open hands and empty bellies
Those whose numbers are massive
Those who seek refuge
From nature's currents and man's resources

Those who are forgotten in the mean times

Those who remember

Ahmad from Guinea makes my falafel sandwich and says
So this is your country

Yes Amadou this my country
And these my people

Evacuated as if criminal
Rescued by neighbors
Shot by soldiers

Adamant they belong

The rest of the world can now see
What I have seen

Do not look away

The rest of the world lives here too
In America

Fasting Food

He barely looks up
Rarely looks away
From the grillthefryertheknife

In the city's ugliest heat
He serves ancestral memory
Tin folied and wraps himself away

There is always Quran as he grinds
There is always Um Kolthom as he grinds

Day begins as dawn is dreaming
Day does not end
He fasts through the rush

He will sleep alone
On the floor in a crowded room
Even when company or bed become available

He can't stand the smell of himself
The looks of others

His clothes his hair his skin
Are saturated with onionssweatcurryexhaustion

Tears never come

Burnmarksdeepcutsachea upon ache

On his hips hang keys to doors
He will never again open

He is lamppost

He is concrete

I place it in my heart his face

When he hot sauces my sandwich unasked

My blood understands
This is how this man
Shows his love

Black Silver

This screen — silver and boxed
Was never meant to carry
black. Even the sound of
dark skin was too loud for
silent movies. Unless you
could smile in service there
was no use for you. Being human
was out of the question. Speak
when addressed to. No home life
outside of white. No love
life unless you loved a white tap
dancing girl with curled straight hair.

Somehow you managed, found
a way to display humanity
and gave butterflies wings strong
enough to higher fly. A glimpse
into a history grander than studio imagination.

And from a contested corner of this silver screen
you managed to spread out black —
in light shades at first, gradually inviting more
color as you took more space.

Not romantic sameness but the differences
that make folks dynamic — the contradictions
and dramas of the lives of people never
meant to tell their own stories.

That butterfly with fodder on her wings
is a phoenix now — multicolored and
magical — inside the hearts of millions
who now see themselves

hear their stories
and want to share their
visions with the world.

So many more stories to tell.
So many more silver screens to paint human.

Kelly Norman Ellis

The Letting Down of Milk

I am standing in the doorway of my kitchen
with morning in my eyes and sleep in my throat
wearing one of Kevin's old Chicago Bears tee shirts
with the cordless in my hand listening to him yell *Wake up girl
the world has gone crazy*! And I am staring at the TV that I forgot
to turn off before going to bed on September 10, the TV we use
for Elmo and Teletubby videos, I am standing in front of that TV now,
listening to Kevin tremble through the phone, and I am watching
airplanes fly into buildings, and all I can think of is nursing
          my daughter.

My daughter hasn't nursed in 10 months. She is asleep in red footy
pajamas with her pink lips slightly parted. I think I must be crazy
because my breasts have been dry for months.

Her first day on earth, my daughter drank from my breasts,
her mouth breaking the tender nipple skin.
My mother-in-law took my finger in her hand and rubbed it
          in the first milk.
Rub your milk in the wound she said *it will heal* she said. And so I
am standing here waiting for that sensation in my nipples
          that would only happen
when my daughter wailed her hunger cry, or when I walked
into a supermarket and heard another baby's willful tears, and I
would have to run before by blouse or sweater soaked though
and find my child's greedy puckering mouth to soothe my ache.

I turn up the sound and hear Bryant Gumble's voice fumbling now.
I want to run down the hall and wake up the baby,
but I don't because I think I must be crazy.
This is supposed to be just another day.

A day for making oatmeal with bananas,
and watching purple dinosaurs on TV,
turning on the dishwasher,
and buying more apples and soy milk,
and meeting my editor for coffee,
and grading more essays
but instead,
I am waiting for the letting down of milk,
waiting for my shirt to be soaked.
And then I am watch skyscrapers accordion into sidewalks
and my mind folds into itself remembering the people I know,
the people I love. Ricardo and Patrick
and Quraysh and Emily
and Onan and Nile
and Ellen,
where is Ellen?

I have wasted so much milk.
All that milk I pumped away,
or that leaked through my bra as I drove down the freeway,
washed down me in the warm shower . . .
gone

Can I have it back?
I must not be in my right mind
cause I am standing in the kitchen
with my hands clutched to my chest
wishing my breasts would weep.

Christine Rose James

Jackfruit Leaves

for my mother

My mother's hands are like jackfruit leaves
so smooth on the outside
when I press their surface to my cheeks
our skins weld to one

My mother's hands are like jackfruit leaves
their underbellies slightly rough and chapped at the edges
when she rubs coconut oil in my hair
my coarse strands seek home in her calluses

My mother's hands are like jackfruit leaves
I can trace the tributaries on all their surfaces
and I will never find an end to their journey
forever winding around the spaces between her fingers
and the expanse of her palm

My mother's hands are the annals of her history
holding a drug addict's fingers as he takes a last breath
folding them in prayer as her husband ties the *minna* around her neck
clenching her fists as she pushes for a new life
wiping her tears as her daughters say goodbye

I can hold my hands next to my mother's hands
and see all the living I have yet to do

Bandit Memory

I stare at your bed
My sheets have fallen in love with your quilt
finding solace in one another's threads
I pull them apart
until their mountains sink into valleys
until your quilt lies on my sheet's back
I let them hug my waist
and curl between my legs
I turn onto my side like a fish
straining against the sand, drained of water
but my limbs are heavy
My fingers skate along the crater in your pillow
climbing out along the strands of silver
I tie a tattered cream cloth under my nose
stretched across my face
like a bandit
I am stealing a scent of you

Frank X Walker

Black Buddha

Sitting back on her own throne, house-shoed and robed
eyes squeezed shut, hands resting on her stomach
she inhales slow and methodically as if gathering
something heavy into a little knot in her belly

slowing letting it rise to her throat, like steam
setting it briefly on her tongue, tasting the last of it
before releasing it into the air with a shutter of relief
of gratitude, of appreciation for her discipline, her

restraint, her hard won victory over her own anger
then she says with a laugh, "I almost lost it tonight son.
This ol' biddy on my ward, too lazy to use a bedpan
saw me walk into the room, waved off the little blond

attendant and said, *I want the little nigger girl to wipe me.*"
I smile, inhale her strength, and let go of my now tiny fury.

The Price of Lamb

After Langston Hughes for Suheir Hammad

What happens to a dream deferred?

Does it crumble like an apartment building
full of women and children
when an Israeli rocket knocks, politely
and invites Arab men out to play?

Does it ricochet like an angry rock
from a child's hand, bouncing off a friendly tank
in occupied territory?

Does it protest silently with tears
like only a grieving mother can?

Or does it kneel and pray
five times a day
that Palestinian people will be free
put on a heavy vest   and explode?

Thirteen Ways of Looking at a Blackman

after Wallace Stevens

I

Among twelve alabaster justices
The only moving thing
Was the fate of a man, black.

II

I was out of my mind
Staring at a tree
In which there were three blackmen.

III

The blackmen whirled in the autumn winds.
None of it was pantomimed.

IV

A mob and a hemp rope
Are one.
A mob and a rope and a blackman
Are many.

V

I do not know which I prefer,
The beauty of jazz
Or the beauty of the blues,
The blackman laughing
Or crying.

VI

Icicles filled their cold hearts
With broken glass.
The shadows of blackmen
Crossed them, to and fro,
The mood
Buoyed by shadows
And incomprehensible bloodlust.

VII

O wiry sons of Bama,
Why do you whistle at locks of gold?
Do you not see how the women, black
Wash the feet
Of the blackmen about you?

VIII

They know the beautiful sounds,
And lucid rhythms of Goodman and Presley;
But they know, too,
That the blackman is involved
In what they stole.

IX

When the blackman disappeared from jail,
It marked the edge
Of several versions of the truth.

X

At the sight of blackmen

Striding in auburn light,
Even at the littlest of them
Did they cry out "eyeball rape."

XI

He toured the South
Driven, of course, in his own carriage.
Once, he was frozen with fear,
After he mistook
An entertainer dressed as a minstrel
For a blackman.

XII

The Mississippi is tapping her feet.
More blackmen's souls must be taking flight.

XIII

It was dark all day
It was storming
And it was going to storm.
The Blackmen hung
On cedar-limbs.

Ellen Hagan

conjwoman

drunk on the bourbon and the sugar cane drunk on the pinacoloda margarita hurricane sexonthebeach fuzzynavel blowjob bullshit we get on every corner southern crawl full on shrimp and grits the okra in the gumbo smooth lost bread oyster po boys from the acme pleasure this act of want slippery insides the water is floating wanna swallow it and chase it the levee breaks anyway beer stays cold from all the ice chests bust open open call cloud of smoke up to my knees now to my waist now can still swallow and wade now

new orleans i have been slow whispering your name i am thinking of you and of us this steady slow grind we do we conjwomen dress all in white carry prayers for marie leveau we women who study the spine of want over red beans and pork chops strut wide open the streets from decatur to rampart swing hips just right trombone trombone slow slide of trombone all whipped with louisiana heat the cat sitting stank in the box of peanut chews at the a & p on the corner settin spells lazy while crawfish boil in a vat of salty garlic water slipping down below the belly of want wanna come back here to you baby travel frenchman street to the praline connection where we eat fried chicken livers and fried pickles and cajun fried catfish cold beer swallow all the hellos swallow all the getting to know you's and slip into all the i want you's we really wanna say anyway

want to take you home mardi gras beads and distance marking the delta to the bluegrass the bayou to the kentucky river meridian to maysville and back again and back again we swim rivers like the first time pontchatrain biloxi ohio the wide of my back stroke ripping the water onto the shore i can feel the beads wrapping themselves round my neck can see your hands stretching can still open my eyes quick out of breath and reaching

Poem #1 / break me

I really need to know why we fall in love with men we know will break us, bones loose and shaking in our skin, rattling. Men who will make our bodies torn and bruised, blue, black, purple. If you hit me enough, I will be every color you want me to be. If you tell me you love me every time after your fingers have punched holes in my mouth then I will start to believe you. I'll believe the marks; believe that you love me. You must. It's too warm to shut the windows. The ocean is loud like a stereo tonight and I can hear it all the way across the bay. You never call and I think you must be in the arms of someone who is not loving you enough. You're in the arms of love, the belly of want, soaking up his love. I want to tell you that I hope he is making you open your mouth, come loud as a fist breaking ribs, scream loud as a porch swing breaking off its hinges, legs spread and wide. gulley. bay. ocean. current. low-tide. gulley. Seaweed wrapped around your hands, handcuffed. I hope your pussy is popping louder than your mouth will be shouting to get the hell out of my house.
You are not a goddamned piece of shit, not a whore because you like it, not a slut, bitch, dumb ass pig. When a man calls you that you are not what he keeps saying. Send him back. Heal bloody, broken bones. Set them straight again. Hold them in place.

Plan B

Plan B the doctor hooks you up.
One prescription.
Two pills.
Three days too late.
Four hairs you pull from your pretty, pretty head.
Five phone calls you've made in two days.
Six times you've cried.
Seven holes in the wall now.
Eight times your fist has ached.
Nine times you've called him a,
"Sick fucking piece of shit dumb-ass mother fucker!"
to yourself.
Ten hours alone, in bed, covers pulled up to your chin.
Eleven times you've pushed your stomach out
in your bedroom mirror,
one time your mom caught you and you said you'd eaten
too much at dinner.
Twelve times you've lied now, to yourself mostly.
Thirteen, your age.
Fourteen days till school starts.
Fifteen hours of watching MTV in one day.
Sixteen ways to kill yourself, and maybe two ways to kill him.
Seventeen magazine arrives today to tell you all the ways
to protect yourself.
You can't depend on one.

Tiffany Midge

What is the Sound of America?

For Silas Whitman and Ron Welburn

Did Chief Joseph hear the dixie-land jazz, the ragtime,
the house parties, jubilees, evangelists
bands playing pentecostol hymns
on hot summer nights? Was he there
during do-wop, the creek river rallies,
syncopation, the grind, that gyration
of hips and spines on a hard-wood floor?
Did he hear, *wow the crowd* on a quarter-acre of heartbreak?
Did Chief Joseph ask: Are you a musican
or an entertainer? Old hymnals transposed to bell and drum,
from old ledgers, and the King James Bible.

Did he speak the language of the later Gods?
Dizzy Gillespie, Coltrane, Miles Davis,
Louis Armstrong, Duke Ellington, Cab
Calloway, Charlie Parker?

This is what happened when the missionaries
tried to convert our heathen souls:
The Lollipop Six, Nez Percians, Jack Teagarden,
International Sweethearts of Rhythm,
Scrapper Blackwell, "Big Chief" Russell Moore,
Dan Beyhylle and the Ten Little Indians,
Junior Walker and the All Stars, Buck
Clayton, Pee Wee Russell, Harry "Fox" McCormick,
Chief Shenatona and the All Indian Band.

What is the sound of America?
The ching-*chinga-ching, ching-chinga-ching*

of brush strokes against a brass cymbal?
A 49'er, *I don't care if you're married*
I'll get you yet, I'll take you home in my one-eyed Ford?
Old moccasinned ladies grinding on a Saturday night?
Horns so anguished they made people weep?
Buglers dodging flying bullets?

Survivance. This is the sound of survivance.

The sound of wind whistling through the Snake River Canyon.
The sound of a stomp dance, bells and seeds.
The sound of "Indians playing jazz."

Her Kind of Horses

Yesterday, I met a Navaho woman with turquoise horses. She said there are rainbow horses, abalone horses, amethyst horses. I wondered what kind of horse carries me through this illusionary labyrinth? Because I live in Appaloosa country, and because I live in the Nez Perce and Lapwai homelands, and because Lapwai means Land of Butterflies in the Nez Perce language, I would guess I am carried by butterfly horses.

Yesterday, I met a Blackfoot woman named Butterfly, *Pepillon,* French for Butterfly. She had a tattoo of a butterfly inked on her hand. She is one of seven daughters who was raised by a rancher. She spent all her Montana summer days as a girl breaking horses, bucking hay, mending fence. I forgot to ask what kind of horse carries her spirit, but I imagine it would be a butterly horse also.

Yesterday, I met an Apache woman who believes in storms. Who has pulled four children from her body like flowers. I wondered if her son Hawk was born or conceived during a storm. I wondered if the storm was male or female. I wondered what stone or winged horses drives her spirit, because she is soft as female rain in the mesas of this glittering world. But her heart is fierce and devoted as the hardest lightning in her loving. She is a hundred kinds of rain, a hundred kinds of storms, a hundred kinds of radiant horses.

Matrimonial Vows for Cannibals

I will forsake all bodies. I relinquish
all other holy, fossiled, recipes of depravity,
the relics and the mummies,
the remains and the newly fattened.

For you, yes, for you.

No snacks, no dishes, no wishes, no rations.

I give up the sphincters, the iris, the corns.
I give up the pinkie nails, the harelip, the charlie horse.
I give up the tear ducts, widow's peak, the sciatic.
I give up the Achilles, the gallbladder, and plantar warts.

It was the knuckles I loved best.
So hard to give up, my darling, but worth it for yours —
each with a rough and scaly patch like broken plaster
and such a knobby dome of glass,
that cartilage poised beneath that dimpled gap.

In each hair follicle I recovered amplitudes, restored vision to the blind.
In each eyelid fold I drove men to kill.
In each clavicle I fought against the snouts of beasts.

Tell me again how you love me, *really, love me.*

I sharpen your bones into knives, carve you into spoons.
I pound your viscera out like a kitchen rug on the first warm day of spring.
I iron out those jowls, that jibbly hang of stomach fat, love-handles.
I wreak fists to nails, scoop and shovel the creosote of your lovely liver.

It is your corpse I love best.
Your tawny hide and wee-wee piggy toes.

Your scrotum's wrinkles, your lip's pretty sneer.
Your useless skin-tags, your elbow's pucker.

Darling, I love the Holocaust of you, the cadaver of you.
I love the splatter of you, the crop dusting of you.
I love the horror that you are beneath the skin.

I love the tail-bone gristle, the oily tallow of shins.
I love the tomato-thick nourishment of your plasma.
The sinewy muscle pulled like red taffy.
I love the violence and the porno of you.
I love the post-colonial imperialism of you.
You are my last supper.
You are my sacrificial offering.
You are my fecundity, my profanity, my solyent green.

and after I make a meal of your limbic spectacle,
and after I chew the heartiest of your rubbery artery,
and before I peel away your hamstring pelt,
I will savor your brain for last, that soft, sweet rind,
your edible, desirable, loveable, mind.

Yael Flusberg

Columbia Road Passover

Safeways in DC used to be known by nicknames
the way kids carry names like
      badges
            armor
                  harikari swords

The Soviet Safeway:
steep shortages, long lines
The Social Safeway:
where the upper crust meet
by the grain-fed meat
still warm baked goods
sweetening the road to redemption.
The Ghetto Safeway:
produce like slimly picked
past-overs from wealthier 'burbs
where we could not get to
unless bused. Fruit flies flipping over
desiccated bodies of soft red onions
like disaster survivors to supply trucks.

In a city within a city that descended
on our sticky sweet dark district nine months
each year, we trusted these nicknames
as truthsayers — never the newspapers'
version of our quality of taste.

This was when summer jobs
were patently accepted patronage perks,
when neighborhood parks were full of teens
parking on the basketball court to reach their high,

of five and dimes
and Nation of Islam bow-tied sentries
patrolling public housing projects.

Then, the Green Line rolled in, speeding up
the greening of the hood.
From divestment leftover from '68
to diversity as a sales pitch
carrying signs of change:
Joggers east of 14th running
from nobody but themselves.
Doggie day care next to chained fried chicken.
Chips and salsa at Mixtec for the Tex-Mex crowd.
Tanning on U in a "Deluxe Building" named for the Duke.
In apartments where tenants were bought out
and billboards arrived proclaiming
"Urban Living!", long-time residents were treated
to outside views of duplexed track lighting
stone sinks, open space designs,
sky high fences, and even, organic edamame
at the Ghetto Safeway on Columbia Road.

It was not the natural products that momentarily
froze me, but four varieties of blintzes,
cheese, cherry, potato and blueberry.
Two aisles over, a new section
displayed products for my early spring
harvest: crispy matzoh and jarred kreplach
coffee with cardamom, candles the color
of snow for benching yarzeit over my dead.

At least some of those I'd resented
for their sudden willingness to submit
to slumming it south of Mason-Dixon,
some whose culture I had whited out
must have been Jews.
More like me than not.

Safeway simply welcomed us as it had earlier
generations of Jamaicans and Salvadorans,
Amerasians and Oromians.

I prayed the newcomers would not be limited
to engaging by emailing missives to neighborhood
listservs on public peeing, proposing private
parking places, tot lots and doggie runs.

I prayed that this Passover would not keep me
enslaved to narrow definitions of who is who
according to what can be viewed in the space
that you can squeeze through cases
of holiday sale items.

In Hebrew, God's everyday name is "HaShem"
or The Name. Some say names dictate destinies,
but I've seen names mark times like red ribbons
that keeps book spines intact
but let the story continue to surprise.

Sukkot*

I can only believe in a God who knows how to dance.
— Friedrich Nietzche

Harvest my senses to
last the season ahead. I
Fall behind like clockwork and
unwind. Supplies of stark nights
draw me into the well of scents
and I savor the four species.

This autumnal equinox
let me be your ritual
your *lulav*. Palms
stretched skyward
toward immortal eyes
of the myrtle. I image a sprig
planted in the corner
by the crematoria invoking
ancestors who watch my unshrouded
pass safely through the mouth
of the willow. I speak softness
into wounded waters. When your words
are cut, the image slits just above
the throat. So I command the coupled
aravot to set the stoves of matzoh-making
aflame, letting a piece of me
spring ahead.

Let me be your pulpy citron
male and female, your evergreen
of *etrogim*, your herb of grace.
Let me exorcise you with incense.
At winter's beckoning, touch me to

reclaim a moist core
bordered by aromatic rind, sweet as surrender
at the witching hour, amidst half-sleeping
shadows spiriting your heart to
the four orchards of paradise.

Wave me in six directions:
To the left, I'll summon strength to unbind you
      listen for love resonating
      in sunflowers toward the rising of the right
ascend to minister meta-sight, then
      ground you down to basics.
Inch me forward to unearth buried beauty, then
      turn back toward
            what you thought was left behind.

Hold me every day, then on the seventh
let me do seven circuits, let me
dance for rain, let me
         dance for you.

---

* *Sukkot* is a seven-day festival that celebrates the fall harvest. The four species involved in a key ritual that gives thanks for abundance (agricultural and otherwise) are the date palm (*lulav*), the myrtle (*hadas*), the willow (*aravah*) and the citron (*etrog*), each of which represent different parts of our bodies, and carry other meanings in Jewish healing rituals. At one point in the ceremony celebrating *Sukkot*, the four species are waved in the six directions, symbolizing wholeness.

Tu Beshvat*

This full moon of nuts and fruits
comes closer to the Chinese New Year
than the vernal equinox, birthing wood from water.

I bless the Tree of Knowledge, of Life
for circulating nutrients to photosynthesized
leaves bearing fruits of the seven species.
I need to yank nothing, slaughter only
dark energy built up over cold long nights
I spent in bed without You.

Wheat, for bread is enough to beget friends
Barley, for a crown like Samuel and Sampson
Figs of truth from the primordial tree
Pomegranate drippings like the scarlet letter
Olives of the salt-craving satisfaction
Dates, of the divinely sweet sex I can't recall.
But, if I take the grapevine's wine,
the red of blood, the white of semen,
perhaps I will fertilize the Earth
with my drunkenness.

---

* *Tu Beshvat, the 15th of the Hebrew month of Shevat, is also known as the "New Year of the Trees" when a celebratory dinner (seder) is held where we eat only things that don't need to be killed, yanked or pulled.*

Back to the Beginning

We return to the beginning, to before there was light,
and it is good, but only after
dancing at the corner of 6th and I,
seven congregants carrying seven scrolls
curbside for the first time
in 50 years, as the Klezmer band plays on.
Some hands clap, others clasp tight
as we snake around scrolls and console ourselves
knowing that, at least on Simchat Torah, *
an ending really does mean beginning again.

We dance in the street, metal fence and police cars
protecting us from traffic, they say terrorists too, since
today in Sinai, another thunderbolt from an exploding automobile
demolishes a golden image of tourists on holiday. These fences
round the Torah don't make me feel any more like a real Jew,
don't make me feel any more like a safe citizen,
but when a woman gleefully shouts
"Excuse the dancing Jews coming through!" —
could that have been my own voice? —
I think I hear G-d saying: And
      there was lightness, and
            it was all good.

Tonight, Moses died again, with only a vision
of the Promised Land.
Before Moses returned from where he came,
he laid his hands on Joshua, the son of Nun,
and Joshua became full of the spirit of wisdom.
Laid his hands like the Hebrew word for ordination,
laid his hands like elders bless little children,
laid his hands like I
reiki friends, palms pulsating into
          epicenters of pain.

Tonight, I dance hoping that the Homeland too
will begin anew like Genesis.
And in one year, Moses will again lay hands and lay down.
Next year, we'll revisit this corner of dancing scrolls, only
we'll be a little changed, and ready to begin again.

*   This poem is about *Simchat Torah* (literally *Joy of the Torah*), a holiday where Jews — who read one chapter of the Five Books of Moses each Saturday in synagogue — get to the end of their collective storytelling and go back to the beginning; that is, they read both the last chapter in Deuteronomy where Moses dies and the Hebrews are about to cross the river into the Promised Land AND the first chapter of Genesis "While G-d was beginning to create heaven and earth...."

Los Bolos *

> *To Dr. Juan Romagoza who recognizes (and treats)
> many "bolos" on Mount Pleasant Street from the time he
> was imprisoned and tortured by them, then-soldiers, in
> El Salvador.*

sit on the corner of Mount Pleasant and
their memories, armed with brown-bagged
bottles of their brotherhood. Waterlogged,
they wander as far as Restaurant Row,
closer to the source of suppers left over,
to other brothers whose wallets weigh
with the warmth of inside
as they hand out loose change

before los bolos pass out in pairs. The cops
start by loudspeaker: *You cannot sleep
on the sidewalk, I repeat, you cannot sleep...*
Their sleep does not have ears, does not wear
striped pajamas and brush its teeth upon
arising. Annoyed, the men in blue will park
their cruisers, prodding the somnolent
with gloved fists and nightsticks.

This is what happens
happily ever after.

Twenty years after war
contestants trade places.
Torturers transform into
the ones on parade
the ones with crusted blood
inches above crudded eyes that see
only another day gone by.

The ones whose flesh form
Babylonian pyramids, whose
shit-covered skin services smut
hallucinations of higher ups, will live
these moments on the corner of their
memories, twenty years from today.

The ones who cock grins for the cameras
are condemned to return to interrogation chambers,
facing a flashlight as they are lifted up, and
into patrol cars while passersby line up
for pasta dinners.

* Los Bolos is Salvadoran slang for "wino"

Making Love Transparent

> *Sage is prayer made visible.*
> — Grandmother Mechi Garza

I want to write about things profound.
About kids flying back from Iraq, missing
limbs or mothers. I want to write about kids
playing hopscotch up the block wanting
to beatbox, like older brothers who instead beat
their souls into small white rocks sucking
swirling smoke since it's surer
than dead dreams. Ghetto rats and rednecks fodder
for a war waged in boardrooms with plush leather
projected onto maps of flatlands, drills and burning
bodies shattering and the sharp screaming.
Instead I blush at the rush I felt
this morning wishing he was with me
in bed, willing his skin to the tip
of my tongue, my flesh folding him in
two spirits encased in soft tissue
turning themselves inside out, making love
                              transparent.

This desire is like a downpour on the border
of ecstasy and despair, doubts drumming
tombstones where nurseries ought to be.
Thoughts swim frantically. *You cannot have
what you want* or *have it but it is destined
to change* or *get it but it will retreat
like a powerful wave destroying
everything in its path.* I declare war
on this desire, dig it a trench
where it can live underground, come
out when a white flag replaces the bloody
one I've found myself wrapped in — a burial
shroud of the wounded — before.

Parneshia Jones

100 Storms of Slaughter

for Rwanda and her people

Photographs of the murdered
hang like lynched doves
in the memorial of Rwanda.

Tombstones line the fields
like strings of pearls in the distance.
This land, lukewarm with blood
has lost its warriors.

There is no one left to kiss
the faces of widows.
No one left to hear the weeping
of women who out live their sons.

Children dance with death
in the killing fields.
Who will forgive the sodomy?
Girls burgeoning wombs laced with AIDS.

Raped in and out of conscious,
they will never laugh again.
They can only watch their graves
being dug on hillsides.

Rwandans pray for forgiveness.
They ask the spirit world for healing.
They try to talk to the ancestors
and listen for their answers.
But their words cannot be heard
in the storm of tears.

Georgia on My Mind

for the children of Atlanta, 1979-1982

Remember us

Mamas and daddies
up all hours
pacing
looking for their missing
angels with mutilated wings.

Kiss our mothers for us.

Some were never found,
their bones swept under moss trees.
Children's cries sweat
on the foreheads of fathers
sleeping with nightmares.

Mothers scream in their pillows,
not wanting to close their eyes
to see the dead faces of their children.

Tell our fathers we love them.

We still search for them,
still believe they will come
back to us smelling of burnt peaches
and baby's breath, fresh and dewy-eyed,
unharmed and happy, we still pray
they will come to us in the night.

Remember us.

And we do,
the lost children of Atlanta.
We remember the sounds of you vanishing,
the sounds of your father's hearts on fire,
and your mothers' wombs bursting.

Sacrifice

for Mabel

How did you learn to swallow
your babies' whole, their bones
crushing your velvet insides.

Mistakes, one night stands,
lying with nameless fathers,
your heart numb to the pain
of unborn sons and whispered faces
of daughters who will never be.

You sometimes waited to the brink
of your second trimester
before you decided to empty your belly,
your womb becoming a grave-site
of fetal ash.

How did you survive cold steel tables
feeding off your uterus and resurrect
yourself to face another day?

Each one aged you ten years,
each one took their place
in memory handing you sorrow.

I was never one to judge or lay blame,
sometimes I drove you to the clinic,
feeling like the accomplice
in the robbery of your womb.

Sometimes I brought you home,
watched you sleep and recover.

I never once questioned if you
were dying inside until you asked

*I wonder what they would have looked like.
I wonder sometimes how they would
have smelled the first time I held them,
what they would have sounded like.*

*I wonder if they would have loved me
as much as I loved all of them?
Will I be punished for leaving them behind?*

You'll never know the hearts
of your would be children,
only the heartbreak of your sacrifice
for the ones you left behind
who go unburied.

Patricia Smith

Heck

for Michael Brown, FEMA

I am not much
beyond buttoned cuff,
swollen blade-scraped cheek,
hair glued flat with tap water, then oiled
for precision. There is always veneer
to be had, an oily English to be borrowed.
All men should be instructed
to run past mirrors,
our eyes should never reach for us,
should never conjure image to be answered.

I am a man, a stacker of clean paper.
Tiny storms inhale my hours.

Looting

The stores are ripped wide,
bleeding unchecked negroes who crumple
under gaudy electronics, balance towers
of hard white Jordans, scream forward
rusted shopping carts crammed to bursting
with nowhere to go. Looters circle and bellow,
circle and howl, trumpeting their felonies,
groaning under bassinets and vacuum cleaners,
balancing big-screens across blazing shoulders,
hurtling for their drowned addresses.
Soggy boxes droop and give,
and — *shit!* — sudden splintered treasure
bloodies ankles, sparkles the boulevard,
stubbornly lights the way.

What Was the First Sound?

it made, heaven's seam splitting?
Was the sound purple?

The sound was purple.
It flashed like a hidden wound
under moving clouds.

Under moving clouds,
a clutched and swollen secret
considered bodies.

Consider bodies,
already filled with water
secure in their bone.

Secure in its bone,
a strong building shit bricks.
The sound was purple.

The sound was purple.
And only brick and concrete
and tree trunks heard it.

Tree trunks heard it
tiptoeing through dying leaves.
Wind was its color.

Wind was its color
casting an eerie no sound
to the first plops of rain

To the first plops of rain,
add the sound of purple,

shitting bricks losing bone,
the seam splitting and finally spilling

bodies

already filled with water.

Character Study

As soon as I scripted a line that blessed him
with a functioning heart, he strode naked
out of my novel, squeezed his squirming head
through the space in a double-spaced line
and gaped at me, eyes wounded by my indecision.
He shoved at a weakened verb and ripped
the prose wide open, bled twisted smell on the keys,
laughed maniacally at the optimistic progression
of page numbers. His huge mouth, having existed
as both empty howl and sputtering door slammed
shut, was crammed with misplaced teeth.
He was nude and ashy, swathed in stiff denim,
his voice base gravel, then rootless and defiant,
his eyes pulsed gray, bottomless black, flat green
with flecks of spittle, his height wavered, his flat
tattooed gut pouted, then didn't. He was scarred
by every change I'd made, every strike-through,
cut/paste, backspace, delete, all the unleased
betrayal that roars through prose. I built him
from a knowing of adjectives, piled on detail
and declaration, and now he is overdone, dragging
all that weight and wheezing when he breathes.
The boy patiently loads his pockets with stones,
bottle caps and jagged pieces of glass, waiting
for the moment when the skin of my neck is exposed.
Only 11, he scans me with man eyes and says it,
claiming my nights, advancing the plot in a way
that can't be undone. He says: *Give me a name.*

Roger Bonair-Agard

Brisbane, 1975

i. Bowler — opening spell

All morning, this blistering heat,
oppressive even for one
black as me, and accustomed
to Carribean sun.

My tail is up, and even
off a short run-up, I am
a rainbow of fire and movement.

Still, not a wicket.
My in-swinger is hostile
and I haven't even rolled
my sleeves up yet.
The batsmen can't touch me.
I have them beaten — all ends up.

In the stands, the sea of faces
burned to a pink under their wide-brim hats
is quiet and confused pretending
they haven't heard
a fine edge, or detected the trapped
stance in the thud of an L.B.W.

ii. Umpire

I couldn't care less how much
this savage hoots and points his finger,
how many screamed *howzats?!*
at what he thinks is an out.

If this boy thinks he will win
an appeal from me with anything
less than licking the stumps
clean out of the ground,
then this black fool
must be more stupid than I first thought

This is our game. We taught
these monkeys how to be dignified
how to play the gentleman's sport,
how to be civilized. They'd still
be in trees if not for us.

Now they want to change the game,
embarrasing our batsmen,
coming to the wicket top buttons
undone, trying to frighten us
with their shiny black chests.

I will show them. We are still
their patrons in this game.
Good white wickets are not
this nigger's, for the taking.

iii. Bowler — just before noon

So apparently, even an obvious
top edge is not enough
to give me my due.

I'm going back to the long run-up
To hell with strategy and field placement.
I'm not even looking for the L.B.W.
or the catch amongst the slips and gullies.

This next delivery will be pressure,
short-pitched
in-swinger
from wide in the crease
up and in at the hapless right-hander
Let me show these fuckers
who is Man here.

If I can't get the wicket,
I'll take the white's boy's head.

To Mimic Magic

> *To the umpires, he was malevolent stealth personified,*
> *so they called him The Whispering Death.*
> Wisden (on Michael Holding)

i. The bowler is a shaman

Even on the black and white
we could tell the ball
was a wicked duppy

it moved furniture
spat and reared at the batsman's
throat shot past his chest
like a comet

the bowler a hypnotist
priest doling out a fiery eucharist
was all our fathers
a silent stern unsmiling man
nevertheless so smooth

we all imitated him
on the courtyard the field the pitch
especially next day

It was the fastest over ever

and none of the batsman's body
armor had prepared him for the placid
mat of a pitch suddenly turncoat
with grass and movement

We took turns practicing
the interminable run-up
the willow of a body gathering
speed and purpose like a train
head ever so slightly turning
side to side
the soft landing of the feet
ball cupped like a co-conspirator
in a bent wrist
each stride a human gazelle's

Dexter was the closest facsimile
we were 13 but he was already
six foot and slightly bearded
he alone had the body to mimic
the phantom ferocity the ninja-like
ability to approach in quiet and leave
a swathe of blood

but we all took turns anyway
giggling after each boy's gambit
and mocking excitedly the jack-in-the-box
twists the batsman needed
to avoid serious injury

Even then we knew we had witnessed
an improbable history
a black man billowing
like a sail in the distance
so fearsome that the batsman kept
his head down until the ship docked
a fierce unfurling of colors in the sun
and an explosion of gunfire
never heard before
We all saw it

We all knew it
but we never called it
by name

ii. *As for the batsman . . .*

No slouch
his *Fundamentals of Batting for Young Cricketers*
was the best selling primer on the subject

Technically gifted
from foot-width to shoulder-placement
he spoke of the high backlift
against immeasurable pace
the low crouch to read
a devil of a googly emerging
like a rabbit from the hat
of a spinner's hand

He was an opener
dealt with the fastest bowlers
on the livest pitches
his history and authority secured
his defenses unassailable

but nothing prepared him that day
for the shiny new ball hissing
like a hot raindrop from the pitch

Twice in six balls his body
arched parentheses into the air
to avoid the missile
while the Bajans already drunk
on Mount Gay rum gasped audibly
at the spectacle

At home we inched our chairs
closer to the TV screen
as if we could shed all the fences
all the limits we didn't know
we had by bathing
in the ball's fiery flight

My mother avoided me
as one would a man
in rapt prayer the altar moving
with each spiteful delivery
and useless attempt at parry

iii. Denoument

By the time Geoff Boycott's off stump
was dislodged on the over's last ball
and jettisoned 20 yards back
he was linked forever
with Michael Holding in cricket lore
in that way that history happens
in the past present future all at once
the way that real history
is poetry in the possible tense
the way all that happens is the rain
and none of us one man's house

We could not have known
even as we started
from our cafeteria or pavilion
or wherever we gathered the next day
how much men and changed we were
school uniforms be damned
accelerating up to the wicket

in fascinated mimicry our flags
beginning to unfurl
our shirttails
blazing

Soul

for Allie and Maureen

Later that night three girls seated
in a row would all say no
to Yuri because he was sweating too much

and later that night i would dance
with Hanz Barbour's sister who was attractive
enough but we danced the slow song
too fast and it meant that i was soft
and couldn't make her grind
her fifteen year old hips against
my thirteen year old ones on the dance floor
and my friends laughed
at me not at us at me

and later that night my mother
would pull up around 2 and blow her horn
outside the party (she and her best friend
Aunty Annette giggling because earlier
they'd dropped me off to my first party
that i was allowed to go to in which
adults weren't involved) and i thought
i was tough and smooth and they giggled
because my friends nodded at me approvingly
because my mother waited until after midnight
to pick me up so my brand new Sergio Valentes
Adidas with the fat laces that Aunty Valerie sent
for me from America were not a waste
and i'd go into the car later that night
and they'd ask me who i danced with
and i must have blushed because my mother
and Aunty Annette were knee slapping dashboard pounding

and had to stop the car in the middle of the street
and there were tears in my mother's eyes
she was laughing so hard and i couldn't
understand why but that was later
that night

after i had acted cool
at most of the right times and danced
well enough and my threads were new
and from America and i had picked
the right moment to ask Lisa Griffith
to dance and had said like my mother
had taught me *May I have this dance* this was
earlier that night before Hanz's sister
Lisa had smiled and the smile lit
her up and her skin was shiny black
and smooth as marble and her eyelashes
were visible across the living room
in the dark of the of the adolescent moon
and she went to St. Joseph's convent
and most of those girls liked boys from St. Mary's
and not those hooligan QRC boys like me
but she smiled and it lit me up and she said yes
Lisa with the baby powder blue dress
with the puffy sleeves Lisa with the perfect
jheri curl Lisa let me hold her against the wall
and grind slow and soulful while Christopher Cross
wailed something about the moon and New York City

That was earlier in the night that year
but after the fight with Lyndon where i got
my ass beat but broke his tooth with
the hardest punch i'd thrown to that point
and the boys gave me dap and said i was a man
earlier that night Lisa said yes and i kissed her
during the dance more out of obligation

than any real physical intent and the girls said yes
almost because the boys had it was early
in the night that year before my grades plummeted

and my mother stopped laughing
and blamed it on my discovering
girls though truth be told
I'd already been fucking
two years before Lisa Griffith
made an acolite of the moon

It was earlier that year
my step-father left
and blamed it on my mother's
not being a good housewife
and not on his red-head secretary
who tried to win me over
with five-dollar bills and free access
to the tennis club

the year she cut up all his clothes
and left them with naked pictures of him
on the front lawn   so i called her
a cunt in the middle of the street
and wore women badly for years

before we all said
*Rog can handle the upheaval
he's the strong one* — me included
so no-one saw me slip
into the funny-man mask like a suit
of armor for the soul and no dance
no song had the power of a mother's
car horn or Lisa's eyelashes or perfect
jheri curls anymore

I shortened the distance
between frustration and impulse
and opened Kurt's forehead with a stapler
and Vanessa del Rio and her three-inch clit
became my hero it was that year early
i started practicing something
meticulous in its denial a fierce grace
that was the year I perfected a complex mechanics
pretending to be a mask the year i practiced
to become a man

Hao Wang

The News

I do not hear
the polite warbling,
the kind musings on my bright and noble future —
instead I peruse the papers:
two twins separated at birth, reunited
after twenty-odd years by some miraculous stroke;
a beached whale off the Oregon coast, exploded
with a few crates of dynamite and a laugh;
a village in the African mess, massacred
and buried, machete and bayonet —
in this circus of irony,
I remember each story for its humor, nothing more.
From the conference room
with the half-open door,
I can hear my father's voice —
he speaks to the counselor
as if dictating a screenplay, knowing each dialogue
and subtle turn of lighting.
He narrates in familiar themes: college, doctor, family.
I remember each word for its severity,
its unimpressionable weight.
She in turn plays her part,
nods and acknowledges my future
like the bicycle thief
bowing to the swarthy officers
on the next page.
I examine a ceremonial handshake,
a photograph of old generals
pacified into smiles and treaties,
and I sense
a knotted chord between father and son

that tenses with each word,
that binds me in questions without answers
like the eyes of starved children
swollen with maggots,
binds me in unspeakable rage
like the first step of the slam dunk,
frozen in sepia,
in the pride of the father
in the frustration of the son.
What good, I say,
what good for him and for me?
Why one and not the other?
Why one and always the other?
Is it a futility
like these firefighters
in the picture, who scaled the dirty tenements
past Philadelphia's 48th Street
to save the families already dead,
who bear a strange likeness to the crew
of the capsized fishing boat from Oshima?
A futility like the hole
over our spiraling planet
that the scientist wrote of in his letter —
a frustration blossoms with each exhale,
each letter we send, each life saved,
each mile we move toward a loved one?
Perhaps that is what my father
is really discussing,
the aimless destinies and repercussions,
everything in future tense,
the disjoint whisper that threads these unrelated stories
into neighborhoods and cities, nations and continents,
mapping the walls and borders that surround us,
the highways and rivers that spread the word.

Sight

My strength
a shattered jar,
I walked
on spirit
alone.
Now and then I felt
the earth
running its rivers
through my head,
each flow and current —
the rampant flood
and the tranquil stream,
smooth delta
and echoed canyon,
the voice of priest
and mother.
From all around
came a bellow
of water,
which I swallowed,
pressed to my liver,
an overwhelming weight,
a dance of molecules
that blinds with knowledge.
And I, being stubborn,
flung my eyes open
like the mouths of two caves,
steadfast in my making
of stone,
and deep down
I heard a hidden river flowing,
carving its infinite caves.

Lessons

I

Learn how to play the piano from an elephant —
to grant the splinters voice,
to gift the broken pegs with the strength
to stand alone — let ruptured strings be the color
of the concerto you are playing
upon the fractured keys, the mess of white and black —

II

Disregard the watermelon bellies,
the faces ballooned with contempt and self-love:
be more like, say, the mosquito — nose for the vein,
complete in its cycle: look for blood less among the many
pedestrians, stargazers, stockbrokers, and malcontents,
but from the one person who will give you life.

III

The cheetah cannot teach you to run the marathon —
it knows not the peopled streets of patience
or the ache of persistence rising up from your tired liver.
But turn your mind to speed, to the whir of city blocks,
the shuffle of wheels and suitcases, the sudden fist
of wrecking balls and taxicabs, the fiddle-tune of tenements
and the barn-dance of satellite dishes and American flags — *then*
seek the spotted cat whose lightning feet astonish themselves

Meditations on a Restaurant Hamburger

Think of the platonic vacancy
of the beast, whose unexamined life
provided in part for my meal.
Mark the absence of questions
and the plurality of grass.
I have read somewhere
that there is no significance
in constant chewing
and dedicated digestion
without purpose.
Nevertheless I have enjoyed
the bovine tenderness
of this soul,
the wisdom of his flesh
that has now passed to me.
Our dialogue is intimate
because is it not this animal
with its clumsy, enormous breath
who now lends me the strength
of everyday life?
So let us say
without pretense
that there is a bond between us,
the cow and me.
Why then should I mourn this creature?
Why should I not celebrate
its limbs and its liver
that others have forsaken
for the manes of horses
and the hearts of men?
Yes, I shall revel
in the cow's brilliant and remarkable blood,
its passionate

erudite bellows
that have been ignored
for the dishonest crooning of birds!
I shall gloat about
its lack of beauty,
the grace
in its wet, sloppy nose,
and the stoicism
with which it approached
the slaughter.

Today

*Today once more
I will try to be non-violent
one more day
this morning, waking the world away
in the violent day.*
    — Muriel Rukeyser

Today once more,
I will try to stay sane.
Another day,
this life we live, breaking the world away
with the tragedies of the day.

I will try to stay sane watching
prisons grow like forests,
my grandmother become paranoid,
my mother lose her job after 33 years.
I will watch imagination suffocate
in coal mines with middle class hope.

I will leave my revolution
on the back porch,
watch children be frisked in airports,
war zones painted in picture books,
recess under surveillance,
lolli pops passed out with crack pipes.

Today once more,
I will try to stay sane.
Another day,
this life we live, breaking the world away
with the tragedies of the day.

I will tuck sanity in my back pocket,
salute soldiers with one hand,
hold their last rites in the other.
I will watch Vietnam repeat itself
and listen to my father weep.

I will carry dead soldiers on my back
who fought for nation relations,
fill their bullet wounds with salt,
stitch them closed with barb wire,
string them along the borders
to keep the nations out.

Today once more,
I will try to stay sane.
Another day,
this life we live, breaking the world away
with the tragedies of the day.

I will watch buildings get taller,
guns grow stronger, souls get weaker.
I will watch when we only touch
the earth to bury our loved ones
then sell it to developers.

I will put gauze over my mouth
when they break through
my common door, search warrant
my house for illegal freedom.

I will watch democracy flirt with dictatorship.
I will watch them put quotas on happiness,
how many times we kiss our children,
blink, pray, cry.

But they can't take my silence.

Today once more,
I will try to stay sane.
Another day,
this life we live, breaking the world away
with the tragedies of the day.

I will hold sanity close like a scarred lover,
speak in future tense, watch Bushes burn,
wash my grandmother's hair for healing,
imagine what my children will look like.
I will say my prayers when I am awake,
when I am watching, out of silence.

Bianca Spriggs

Salt Skin

In the photograph she is always looking back
with one hand about to flip ginger hair
over her shoulder.
The other clutches at the surface
of a red, plastic keg cup.
Her gaze we follow
to the nigga in the corner.
He is wearing a dress shirt
un-tucked and slightly wrinkled
slinging Spanglish with his boys.

She absorbs him in with the
angles of cornflower irises,
batting shimmer and ash shadowed lids,
tongue perforating lips
glossy with beer residue and name brand.
Her halter is pale gold.
He has noticed her scent
in the same photograph.
Sheared, bald head cocked mid-sentence
as the whiff of her pun-pun over the press
of collegiate flesh, he breathes in.

In the photo, she notices first
his fighter's shoulder breadth,
high, taut ass and the threats in his hands.
He later confesses his pugilistic flings
with violence.
Aroused,
she will ask him to refill her cup
again and again.

Each time he walks away,
she will adjust bra strap and panty line,
ready to become trendsetter
among her friends.
So, she spares only one look back
as he returns with the foamy, full,
red plastic that matches
the hue and gloss of her lips.

In this snapshot,
there are no words
for the way her brew-soaked skin
will tremble in the umbra
of his fingers and tongue
as he divulges and disintegrates
her secret place.
There are no words that will match
the sensation when he plunges in.
Embedded,
he fails to notice the fragile nature of her peach.
Draws blood as she moans and writhes beneath him.
She looks back again, turned on
by his exertion and seed scent.

We will not see her immobile
and exposed next morning,
the way we do that night in a photograph.
We will not see her standing pillar-like
looking back over her flesh
that is now the color of the salt
you melt garden slugs with.
We will not see ash and shimmer,
coloring the skin under her eyes
in shades of bruise,
the swollen teeth marks around her nipples
and navel or the disarray of fluid-soaked

ginger pubic hair.
We will not feel the evidence of shredded
vaginal lips.
We do not see in a thousand words
worth of night vision her lust-punctured tonsils
and unsteady clutch on her cellular phone
as she looks back again over her shoulder
at the sleeping nigga on the bed
and utters words
like *violated*, *drugged*, and *rape*
in a whisper while crouched
in a corner of his room.

In the photograph,
there is never foresight such as this.
Only the almost toss of ginger hair,
an un-tucked dress shirt,
eye shadow of shimmer and ash,
and lips glossy
like the red, plastic cup in her hand,
as she always turns for the first time to look back.

Except Thou Bless Me

On Sunday mornings
I dress alone
in a room behind the baptismal pool
before the congregation arrives.
Sister Alice does the same for evening service.
It is someone's rule
that we serve
clothed in all white.
Dresses with snap buttons,
shoes with Velcro straps,
stockings,
even our slips and lace caps
must be an unblemished white.
We serve water
from pitchers for members of the pulpit.
We move around freely
but silent when we wear the white.
We are pristine and untouchable,
the handmaidens to men of God.

Before this Sunday morning's service,
he comes to me again.
I just ask him not to wrinkle
my whites
before I have to serve.
He doesn't,
but leaves part of himself
on the skirt and hem of my dress instead.
Since I have only one
I have to borrow one of Sister Alice's dresses
that fits too loose on me
and hope she don't notice.

When Alice comes to find me
some Sunday mornings later,
the sermon is half over
and none of the ministers have seen
any water yet.
I am still in my white slip
and fell out, right cheek stuck
to the antique tiles
of the bathroom in the upper room.
She is breathing loudly
because of the climb upstairs
but manages to ask me,
How come inside the toilet look like that?
I tell her,
Because God don't like miracles
He don't have a say in.

She helps me into my whites
and puts a pitcher of water
between my palms praying ceaselessly.
She is a loud prayer.
I feel like I am leaking
all the way down to the altar.

On Sundays, we dress alone
in a back room
out of the way of the congregation
in all white
for morning and evening services.
We pass them laundered linens
that soak up their sweat.
We serve fresh water
from crystal pitchers to whet their tongues
so their sermons won't be dry
as stale marrow.
We are so careful
not to spill a drop on their pulpit floor.

Surface Tension

The skin of it
was already decaying
and tender like the rind
of a tangerine wasted with rot,
still brisk with citrus brine and sweet,
yet, now engorged by a hoary mold.

I wolfed it down anyway
upon seeing her
made big by his seed pearl.
And all the shit I been
talkin' bout being gracious
'cause I got the man
slid away resin slow
and died like a wine jinn
for want of sodden wishes
in my mouth.

And when finally she broke water,
my sloppy chamber pulsed
algorithmic embers hazy
through a hairline crack
that eventually grew up
to open as a whore's supple
mouth might.
Felt my spine upheave
and part ways like a Jericho column.
Buckle and split
the way I imagine
her calves and thighs must have.

This is the way
to become midwife to mourning:

cram in hot sticky white pills
until they overlap
around my own hollow womb
like the pale scales of a koi
kept in a tea tin,
then drift,
stale blossoms or filaments of soot
that sift away from an altar
to some local god.
Sealing off my secret place,
they forbid the offering
of my bleeding season to him.

Couples Skate

And this is how he holds me:
we are hinged at our left palms,
our wheels rise and fall
on waxy, scuffed Palace hardwood
in a syncopated strum
I recognize later
as merely acoustic and hollow.

The disc jockey plays
Time of My Life,
and the skating rink is mostly clear
now, but for children
and their sweethearts,
as shaky legged as foals.
But my father and I,
oh, we are the most confident.
No awkward hand holding,
we cascade with ability,
can even turn
and go backwards together.
We skate in cursive.

My face, like my sister's face,
is painted up as a butterfly
at the rag wrinkly hands
of the woman who sags like an old tent
in a corner of the rink next to a lamp.
Every week, he pays her to trace the dark
circles under our eyes away
into figure eight wings
with greasy brush after brush
illuminating them in fluorescents.
She pauses only to flick

thinning horsehair tips
into baby food jars
of paintmurk and water.

Later, he keeps keepin' time,
repeating how men must always lead.
But, then, he has spotted *her* again,
the red-headed woman
in the dark teal skating outfit
with the short-fringed skirt.
I see her too, now.
She wears white,
high-booted skates,
legs flashing without modesty
a strawberry yogurt pink.
During our slow-dance slow,
skated pirouettes,
he releases me,
suddenly spins me off
towards my sister
who is stumbling around
in the kiddy rink.
He lets me go
at song's climax
for *her*,
as the neon slick
butterfly on my face
begins to bulge and splinter.

Chow Time

Round the corner from my studio apt.,
my driver's side front tire
sighs apart
at two-thirty in the morning
in February,
a whistle away from a Great Lake.

My lover,
hungry and bleary-eyed from the cat,
hustles out of passenger's seat
in down jacket, jeans and sneakers,
to manhandle my little car
onto the spare doughnut
while I hand him lug-nuts
and steep in shiver.

A woman walks her chow.

Two drunks fresh
from club meat market careen by.
That's a big dog!

You two are big assholes!

Watch me piss on your dog!
(punctuated by a grip on his crotch)

You won't do shit,
I'll kick your ass!

Crackwhore, crackwhore!

She pursues *them*,

dragging the chow
who has just begun its business.
My lover with tire iron in hand,
makes it in time
before she lands the first blow.

*Sis, sis it's not worth it,
let them go!*

It took only a few seconds
for her to realize
he was standing in her way.

Fine,
I hear him say,
*Take your beating on your own time.
The last thing I need,*
he tells me,
*is for cops to show up,
and me with a tire iron in my hand
and some white lady screaming at me
to leave her alone.*
We laugh a little sadly,
our chuckles choked
by the Midwest winter's night air.

The woman is now
chasing the drunk men,
punching at them,
slapping at them,
kicking,
falling.

They hold her head
while she swings
and laugh.

Crackwhore, crackwhore!

Tonight must have been the night
she was daring the wrong cat
to say something,
anything to give her an excuse
to kick their ass,
I say as we pull away.

The car wobbles on the driver's side,
and in the rearview
the chow is still trying
to bend in the frozen grass at its knees.

Matthew Shenoda

Voices from the Rubble

I am through with this earth
and its twisted roots
wringing our veins
the soil has molded like wheat
frosting our vision and taste
every street has run counter to our travels
our hearts have been drained into the seas.

It is time for us
to dig
unearth the earth from itself.

Reality

what we have killed in this world
will rise up against us
grass will stage rebellions
in the shape of banana plantations
children will hold council
on the edge of garbage dumps
floating like plastic ashes

the water will overcome us
& our dignity will be perched
in the delta of mangrove branches
palm bark will cover our feet from shame

the mason has called to his children
his tile work the scales of fish

learn to shudder in this life
shake the pollen from your hair

his daughter's eyelids gnarl into finch songs
& thread water with the nurture of understanding
she stands beside her mother
conjuring dawn
they sing the songs of redemption
their verve feeding fig groves

I remember being a child
in coyote hills & whitecap beaches

I remember how men swung chains
in the face of fear
trying to combat the cardamom sun

Maria Blackhorse

Mother Love

I lay my bones down
          upon the earth
 strength gone
      surrendering
to her care

I lay my bones down
          upon the earth
 her great bulk
    cradling me
        soothing me
a beloved child

I lay my bones down
          upon the earth
tears flowing
     unrestrained
         accepted
 like a gift

I lay my bones down
          upon the earth
     quieting
she sings me lullabies
    cooling the fire
       behind my eyes

I lay my bones down
          upon the earth
       listening
to the voices

            of all my relations
    their lyric melodies
            filling the empty places
    inside of me

I lay
    my bones
            down
                upon the earth

I rise
    up
        renewed

Power Song

I am beauty
    gather round
I am speaking
    hear my sound
I am walking
    on this ground
All is beauty
    all around

I am beauty
    gather round
I am praying
    hear my sound
I am sitting
    on this ground
All is beauty
    all around

I am beauty
    gather round
I am singing
    hear my sound
I am dancing
    on this ground
All is beauty
    all around

I am beauty
    gather round
I am listening
    to your sound
I am rooted
    to this ground
Joy lives in me
    I am found

Anne Shelby

Kentucky Junction

That intersection you're asking about —
what was it again? Gender, Politics
and Culture? Yeah — I know where that is.
Round here we just call it The Junction.
First, you go down the middle of the road
a long time, then turn hard to the right —
like a certain party that bulldozed through,
sideswiping school buses, flattening
community centers, crippling every
environmentalist that got in the way.
Ran one gay couple right off the road.
Never even stopped. Big white limousine.
You'll go past the house where the elderly
gentleman lived. He had to go
to the nursing home when they cut out
the meals-on-wheels. Go on past the house
with the flag in the yard and the yellow
ribbon on the mailbox, on past
the boarded-up hardware store that closed
when ConSuMoreMart opened on the bypass.
Don't take that turn at the gravel road.
There's meth labs hid in the woods up there
and it's not safe, unless you're a regular
customer, or a law-man on the take.
Around the bend is the Brand New Old Time
One True Church of the Chosen People,
The One and Only Holy Word, and the
Spiteful, Capricious and Ethnocentric
God. (Women Must Keep Silent —
and something over their heads.) Drive by
quick as you can. Climb the hill. You're there.

This is where it all comes together.
They say that here, on top of this ridge,
Daniel Boone once stood — or maybe
Davy Crockett — gazing westward
over the oldest mountains in the world,
the hills and valleys, forests and rivers,
this New World Paradise, where Cherokee
hunted for a thousand years, and said,
"This way, boys. Better get started."
You'd best hurry, too, if you want to see
The Junction. Of course you can always
find it somewhere else. Not this one, though.
Big coal companies bought up all that land
and the legislators to go with it.
They aim to start blasting in the morning.

Mitchell L.H. Douglas

Another Season

Christmas Eve, when my car breaks down
& reconciling is a New Year's resolution, I arrive

in a tow truck, see the white car parked
where mine should be, choke

on the throb of a beaten heart.
      Inside, I step, stop, feet one

with wood floor, watch two
stir the kitchen's cold air

with slow, warm words.
                      I take a bullet

like Rimbaud — not through the wrist
not just betrayal but failure

of once, of was,
what is   if.

Plastic

There is something to be said for this,
how once freezer bags are emptied,
                        she washes Ziplocks with dishes, hangs

the flat & empty on stoneware backs.
When what was is forgotten,
she fills the bags again, protects goulash

from gray beard, turkey bacon from turning jerky.
She counts pennies, blessings, masters the art
of the scrape.

One night, when the dishes were done,
I thought of how she gives without condition,
                                  proposed without a ring.

Lineage

I. George at the Shimmy Shack

George & his boys are moving,
working that crowd silly

after a day of *Yes sir, No sir (Lord,*
                          let me find a way).

George's horn the rooster morning,
sunlight swath in a midnight juke

standing on the will of God.
The frame, an impossible heap,

leans like lovers for George's solos —
sways for a good breeze. Benny

takes a button to a washboard,
scratches out a scattered heartbeat. Stretch

leans back long, curls his fingers
'round a tight wind of twine

anchored in an overturned tub. A day's work
becomes song. *Yes sir, no sir,*

have a nice day. Yes sir, no sir. Gotta find a way.
Night riders pass, watch hands clap,

hips swing from shadows on horseback.
As much as they love to burn — crosses,

churches, spirits — they never lay a finger
on that shack, just steady the horses, listening.

II. Once

Selma has me cutting apples this morning,
warming walls with brown sugar, cinnamon,

anticipation of melting snow. Once
the thaw outside begins, the thaw inside

will rise, run as sweet as the simmer
I spoon upon my plate.

                I wish there were biscuits, blessed
with the roll & pat of Mamie's hands, grandmother

of Southern soil, schooled in spells of food & fire.
Great Grandma Leola had it too,

the way she waved us in from gravel
to her table, raised pitchers of Coca Cola

cut with orange juice, poured a sweet muddy river
into mason jars.
         When Daddy George returned from the Navy,
raised a fuss over moving to the back of the bus,

Leola said his brothers scoured the Alabama
for his body, feared the night riders revenge

when supper time came & his seat was cold.
        I pictured that river, cloudy

as the juice in my jar, gripped the glass, focused
on the bottom — turned my eyes to lanterns.

III. He put his horn down

where the hogs take corn,
in the toss of dried feed
chickens peck from scorched grass,

on the Alabama's banks
in the secret of the current,
ruse for dogs & riders
mad for black blood,

in the weed patch by the Shimmy Shack
where he blew his lips worth
while liquor poured & spit-shined shoes
stomped the wood plank floor.

He put his horn down

for a one-way bus to no one
where knowing no one
was just fine.

IV. Offerings

Grandfather, 79, scales basement steps,
separates colors & whites
while you say *I can wash my own.*

Grandmother, 80, reads romance novels
like morning papers, sings gospel
with God's soul, precious notes.

Breakfast, toast points
pierce north, east & west,
George Washington, Mamie Lee & you.

Coffee instant, bacon fried long,
grits loose — a hard-boiled egg
rocks the edge of the grains.

Two smiles sip heat from chipped cups,
insist you have seconds.

Debra Kang Dean

"of thee I sing"

> [B]efore release of composite sketches of two John Does, there was a widespread assumption, fueled by media speculation, that the horrific act in America's heartland had to be the work of Middle Eastern terrorists. People on the street talked about their renewed suspicion of foreigners. One called the bombing a declaration of war, not unlike Pearl Harbor.
> — David Maraniss, *The Washington Post*

> "Don't be upset, Jose Alberto. I'm only crying in English."
> — Elizabeth Bishop in Brazil

Not long after news of the Oklahoma City bombing broke,
I thought, *It's déjà vu all over again!* the grief in my throat
like acid reflux, what could I do

                                        but laugh. I thought
of a friend's mother in Michigan, part of a group
of Arab-Americans *large enough to constitute a minority.*

When he and I first met near Ōsaka, Americans hadn't yet topped
critical mass; people were curious. He was free
to be thoroughly American,

                                      getting a waitress's attention
by playing a cowboy accent for all it was worth: "Sue-me-
maah-sin," he'd say, or "Auh-re-gaah-toe" — then break

into real Japanese, fluently casual, unlocking
the waitress's eyes from mine, turning her mouth
(half-frown, half-grimace)

                        into a smile. There,
he didn't mind being a foreigner. I, on the other hand,
till a sip of beer or my native tongue betrayed me,

could and liked being invisible. But I confess
I sometimes sought out "modern" restaurants just to listen
to American music.
                        I once watched him close the distance
between himself and a group of schoolboys working up
the nerve then chanting, "Gaijin, Gaijin"; and he starting to hop

and sway from side to side, keeping their rhythm,
his arms tense and shivering in mock delight,
then advancing, pointing,
                        chanting back,
"Nihon-jin, Nihon-jin," running, the boys
craning their necks backwards and squealing.

Having been talked into taping and watching reruns
of "Cheers" and packing more than once from the States —
nearly half way 'round the world,
                        in fact! — bagfuls
of Combos, boxes of Pop Tarts, I know why
he makes a model of Sam Malone. Incorrigible

womanizer, he translates that challenge into charming
free meals from strangers — and friends, too.
I knew his game
                        and liked him in spite of it.
Sometimes what comes back is the sound
of his feet shuffling against the tiled walk

as we made our way through a mall near Takatsuki
Hankyu-station. I pause to look back, see his wrists,
limp above his pointy
                        elbows, and, on a day

neither of us knows what to make of our lives,
he's leaning against me, saying, "Carry me."

But it's recalling the incongruity and utter compatibility
of the last meal we shared before I stopped
my transpacific visits
       that turned the weather forecast
into background noise: before us on the table,
a dozen dishes portioned in servings no bigger than

a mouthful, weird compromises of Eastern and Western
cuisine whose names escape me — I know it's wrong
but I want to say "enoki pizza" or
         "Texas-style sushi"
to give you the flavor of it. To my grazer's delight,
we ate and ate, keeping each other in beer

in a country where only the intemperate pour their own,
where this simple act could mean, "Here, your glass
is nearly empty" or "Please,
       my glass is nearly empty" —
and talked until he turned, as I knew he would,
to the question he would ask me each time I met him:

"After so many years, aren't you tired of living
with the same person?" Outside the glass wall
of the restored
       eighteenth-century structure,
its thatched roof weathered but intact, was a garden
so carefully constructed, it seemed perfectly natural.

And a tiny waterfall. And under the waterfall,
a bamboo dipper — the kind you might see at temples —
that filled then see-sawed empty,
      Clunk . . . clink,
then started to fill again. Pointing, I said, "It's like that."

Punchbowl

The light that puts out our eyes is darkness to us.
                              — Thoreau

Here in this theatre under the stars,
    Ernie Pyle's marked grave is only one
among thousands simply marked "unknown."
    But long before they were all killed
    along the PacificRim, another drama unfolded,

    a bleak reminder of what seems
        the unkillable law: some thing must die
that others might live. Here was the place
of sacrifice, the bodies of law breakers,
drowned below in a pond, borne up to the crater

and placed on a stone slab — some left alone,
    some reduced to ash and bone that the family
gathered up and carried home. On the slopes
      of this crater, I saw the after-effect of slaughter
    on a small scale — some mongoose or stray

    had found its way into my brother's pigeon coop
        and scattered the flock that never came back.
Memory blinks, and the smell of pigeon shit, blood is
    conjured up, the featherless skin of hatchlings turning
rubbery where they hung on perches or fell.

The road to the now-locked gate branches off to
    "homestead" land, so called so we can forget
the place. They say the crater's extinct,
      the Pacific plate grinding steadily northward,
    but who can really know or say for sure what stirs

      under the surface? The inexorable law of bodies
         tells us no two can occupy the same space.
Some must leave that others might live. *Go back
    where you came from*. But there's no there there
to return to. Tonight I have climbed from my father's house

up over the rim and descended into the crater to lie,
      sober, among the dead. This glimpse of the past —
it's like looking at stars: Once you know what you're seeing,
         the hour of innocence is past. The light of dying stars
      puts out our eyes. Again and again in the dark,

    we stumble. We stumble and fall. And yet,
as if certain we know where we are, we get up.

Adrian Matejka

Cannibalism

I don't worry my head
about what Booker T.
Washington says

because I'm a pure-blooded
American of the first
rate. Colored folks always

been on this land. We
were here before
the United States

was dreamed of.
So I don't need to cast
my bucket unless

there's no indoor toilet.
I know some whites
find my race unappealing,

but they are like weevils
in the good cotton:
always casting reflections.

After the Great Storm,
the *Times* called us "black
ghouls," cannibals eating

colored and whites
like Sunday chicken.
Leaving babies in the streets

of Galveston to take
a dead man's glad rags.
Sawing fingers off at the fat

meat for rings. I was there,
so I know what's true: whole
neighborhoods of coloreds

shot down by whites.
"Protecting the dead"
the sheriffs said,

sending buckshot at every
colored in sight. The dead
didn't need any protection

other than the rocks and mud
they were underneath.
After that storm came

through, me and some
of the other Galveston boys
slept where we could,

spent days searching
for the living. We got paid
whiskey and potatoes.

We found dead mothers
and sons, dead cats
and teacups cracked

like skulls under the wet
wood and rock. That's
all the hurricane left.

"Carefree as a Plantation Darky in Watermelon Time" *

Somehow, I'm a 2 to 1
underdog to Jim Jeffries,
the four flusher who only

retired as champion
because he kept dodging me.
He spilled he wouldn't fight

a colored, but he fought
colored before he was Champion.
Old Jim even worked

the corner when I fought
his brother Jack. Jim saw up
close how Little Jack dropped

like a cherry from a tree
in the fifth. Just like I told
the reporter he would before

the fight. It's not my color
that troubles the man.
It's my left hook

and knowing a colored
would be champion.
I'm going to make a whole

lot of money betting
on myself. If I felt any
better, I'd be afraid

of myself. I'm so fast
I only got my shadow
to spar with and most times,

it don't keep up, either.
So I shoot craps
to train my fists. I play

the fiddle to train my eyes.
I play baseball to get
ready for bed. When

I drive my Flyer over
the red rises into that Reno
sunset, everybody from

Philadelphia to Australia
can see Jack Johnson's taking
his motor car for a ride.

---

*   Description of Johnson training to fight Jim Jeffries for the
Heavyweight Championship.
    — from the *Baltimore American,* July 2, 1910

White Women: Lola Toy

Woman, you are
as delectable and powdered
as beignets.

Your skin, white
enough to catch
a bit of sun

in its own sugar
and hold it
until sweat glints

like a ruby.
Don't you hear
me talking,

pretty momma?
I can play the cello
for you if it'll make

you feel right.
Or you can just keep
on visiting my sparring

exhibitions, keep
covering your mouth
with a gloved hand

like a dove's wing
as you whisper
to your friends.

Did you tell
them the snappy
left that closed

my partner's eye
was for you?
Did you whisper

the gut hook
that dropped him
to his knees

like a sinner
meeting with Death
was for you?

Lee Newton

Invitation

My uncle bowed to the young stewardess
who had been politely serving him Coke
and peanuts during his connecting flight —
noticing one last time her yellow hair,
fair skin, narrow waist. His dark black hair
stood out in the long corridor of blonde,
brown, and gray. It was obvious he began
to change before leaving Korea: new suit,
leather luggage, haircut. His excitement
spilled into conversation during our drive —
silhouettes, neon signs, those pink buildings
lining the 4-lane strip home. He was thirsty;
asked me to stop, the *Purple Panther Club*.
The loud music and bass freed his hands;
the dancer on stage grabbed his attention.
Dressed in a sequined bikini, she wrapped
herself around a pole, legs spread wide —
open like an invitation. He wanted to sit
near the stage, hadn't yet learned the rules,
how to read her eyes, "look; don't touch."
I led us away. She had his attention
again — stripped, unveiled her tasseled breasts,
spun into a white cloud of smoke and mist.
He couldn't keep from staring, his eyes wide
and round. We began to talk of home
and homelands — his, mine, how some things
have changed and how others never will.
I have been here too long; my eyes water, burn.
He wasn't about to leave. He likes it here,
mesmerized by the breasts and thick smoke,
the shiny tassels, loud music, and mirrors.

Everything Broken

Tigers, mother-of-pearl and teak pagodas, marble swans, china tea sets, jade, and ivory: this was my house at twelve. Everything in its own place — perfect, settled, complete. My mother surrounded us with the figures, myths of her homeland. She had carefully packed each piece in newspaper and cardboard, bringing only what would fit neatly in her suitcase during each trip home. The rest, my grandfather mailed in wooden crates from Korea — the boxes simply labeled *pieces, USA*.

Every possession was infused with the spirit of my grandfather, his father, and those who created them. I used to lift the arched piece of ivory from its velvet brace and stare at each figure carved into its side, telling myself a story: those gates before the mountains, the entrance to my home; the little turtle the creature I was to be wary of on dark nights by the lake (he would carry me, separate me from my family if I didn't listen to my mother — that's what she always said); the many houses surrounding the compound, the homes of my grandfather's fourteen wives and mistresses — this part is true; the shapes were separate, distinct, all melding into one beautiful carving.

The moment the vase came crashing to the floor I ran knowing my mother would follow. I waited seconds, minutes, half hours, hours: every part of an afternoon. She never did and I felt safe going downstairs to piece it back together. I examined each porcelain fragment, the brushed Korean characters — our family tree — stopping at my mother's marriage. When she sat down behind me I thought I could feel the sting of her hand on the back of my neck. Again, she did nothing, so I cried. *Why you cry?* she asked. "I've broken your vase, the one grandfather sent you." *No matter; vase already broken.* And when I didn't understand, she flipped through the pieces, found the one with most of her father's name, placed it in my palm and rose to walk away. *Nothing whole; everything broken. Better you realize now than later.*

The Unbroken

My mother — hungry, wearing her brother
on her back — begged the American G.I.s
for food, canned peaches, stale crackers,
things I've never seen her eat. She hid
in barns, watched soldiers line-up
families for execution, always infants first.
She waded through paddies, watched
the stalks, whipped by wind, dip their heads
into water and snap back to attention
shaking off the frequent drowning.
That was fifty years ago. There was a war
going on then. My father wasn't in that war —
too young, only eleven. He was busy
firing his thumb at imaginary Nazis
left over from the Third Reich and arcing
Alabama pines until they burst, broke apart.
My mother — she never broke,
not when the Korean War separated her
from her parents, not 14 years later
when my father brought her home,
not even when my drunken uncle
bent and twisted our family with gales
of racist commentary and hatred.
No, she never broke, but my father did —
severing in two, when he threw his brother
from the porch and swore he'd kill him.
Didn't he have the right to break
this once? I could tell you, in weakness,
he did. But I know better, I know
there's a strength and honesty to be found
in my mother's meek and difficult life;
I know to break is to remain broken.

A Language Lost

for Cliff

We think we know everything
there is to know about our mother.
How she tucked her younger brother
into her narrow side, made two shadows
into one, and slipped through the nights
of the Korean War like a distant yellow star.
We've both been told how, years later
and against her father's wishes, she fell
in love with a big-nosed American
soldier — the distance to her old home
measured by oceans. I have never told
you how she would read to me in English
every night; how, for me, she labored
over every new word, R's, and L's;
how I grew up thinking the silly monkey
in the ballcap and yellow sweater was named
Cool-Ass George. When you were born,
12 years later, her sounds had been smoothed
out; her English par with mine — we had
a common language. Little brother,
we have never had to struggle with letters
or pronunciation. But ask yourself,
now that you are older, what was it
she screamed at the North Korean soldiers,
and if she were to repeat it today,
why is it we wouldn't understand?

Why We Make Love

It's a Baby Boom, of sorts,
this generation, the 200 born
in one month at Fort Campbell,
the 350 conceived at Fort Bragg
when their mothers and fathers
returned from deployment.

I include my twin sons
born nine months after September 11
when I look at them and know, sadly,
they weren't planned, not even
the faintest of considerations.

Maybe those are the best lives —
those who fall into this world
unexpectedly, some beautiful
perennial, unannounced and staking
its claim in the Spring garden — maybe.

Because of me and people like me,
I worry, still, question what will occur
decades from now. Wonder what happens
one morning when they sit at their tables,
ankles crossed, flipping through the *Post*
or *Times*, their fingers painted, stained
with speculative theory, academic conjecture.

What will become of us when they learn
they were not created out of love, lust,
even infatuation, when they discover
so many of us fell into arms and cold beds
out of some primal, instinctual necessity?
What, when they determine they are merely
a product of our sorrow, guilt, and fear?

Maybe it is then we will find ourselves
in a revolution — this angry generation
forcing us to confront our inabilities
to cope, to handle life. Or maybe
they will just stop, stop on the porches,
decks, stand there — newspapers rolled
and under arms — finally understanding
the frailty of our species, the clutter
and confusion of their own lives.

Sabotage

How long? This dance with myself
through the tripwires, the flittering
and brushing of dust-covered mines;
how long before the shrapnel
in all its vibrant intensity and sharpness?

I've never been in love with peace,
with the suburbian complacency,
the rote and routine I've strived to create.
This must be what death feels like.

I love the whole hair-pulling production,
the hands on your collar, my collar,
grandma's china plates against the wall,
fuck, man, this is what life is all about
spectacular spectacle of things.

So how long before I ignite my pretty life,
explode through that frosted-glass window
with all the departmental skeletons,
or sleep with the graduate student who leaves
me notes scented of thrust and passion,
the one who flashes her white cotton triangle
hidden beneath her always too-short skirt?

How long before I feel that rise of anger,
argument, and frustration, before my body —
finally opening to itself and its life —
with its increased heart-rate and flushed skin
tells me I'm alive, I'm alive?

Egrets on the Pond

i.
     It isn't true
they asked to be here.
They'd prefer the coast,
even settle for a deeper
south. Nor is it true
they arrive willingly;
but they come, nonetheless —
year after ending year —
staying for months at a time.

ii.
     I've fished this pond
before, know its emptiness
and voids, the eroded banks
like pitted bark, the stench
of a promising harvest gone
sour. This is my home, though
I've never bothered to call it so.

iii.
     I'm wondering
if there isn't something
to be learned from them.
The way they make the most
of it — standing on stilted
legs searching the depths,
their black eyes staring
with clarity into blacker
water, the grace and ease
in which they step through it.

Some Men Do

I don't know a hell of a lot
about amperes, volts, or currents —
other than they're an invisible force
we have to contend with daily.

This I do know.

Power lines weigh heavy upon themselves;
filled with shocking news they droop
weepingly towards the hard ground.
That stout, strong backs of pine poles
can't sustain the weight for too long —
begin to weaken, splinter, crack —
before they must be relieved of their burden.

And you should know this to be true:

some men stricken with grief
lie heavy, sag in the middle,
and weep, waiting for someone
who's seen it all before
to arrive with two sturdy
pines and prop them up.

Luis Urrea

There Is A Town in Mexico

for Kim Stafford

There is a town in Mexico
where no one ever dies, and the few
who have died did it elsewhere, then
pass through the town square
on their way to the fruit market where
hibiscus flowers bleed red nectar
into tea, mangos are free,
where alamos and olmos trees
are whitewashed halfway up
the trunk, and those few dead
our world has coughed out stop
by a bench where my grandfather
sits at a wrought iron table and
a black Olivetti and a stack
of onionskin bond. "Name,"
he says as he rolls the sheet
into the hungry machine.
And those few dead who wander
in past sugar cane, agaves
spiked dusty jade, snapping turtles
in the spring, the burro's fence,
scratch their heads, unable
to remember their names. "Any
name will do," my grandfather
tells them: for instance, he
calls himself Hummingbird.
He calls John the Baptist
Juanito, and if Emiliano
Zapata ever came down from the hills,
He'd get a new name too. The dead

call themselves Honeysuckle, Xochitl,
Midnight Wind, Coyote.
My grandfather types. Once
they've signed the page,
they scoop a cool cupful of water
from the tiled fountain, shade
their eyes for a minute, and stare
at all those gold shining coins.

Walking Backward in the Dark

So, the jury says, once upon a time you fed the poor.

You couldn't see the ground for the wreckage.
If the women had dysentery behind their sheds
the earth turned green and red and yellow
and you couldn't tell what was food and what
was shit and all your Jim Morrison songs
were without avail. No prayers in your head
took the smell. The only relief was the smoke.
Tijuana's dead dogs, flat cats, starvation cows
and highway horses split open by retired
Illinois Macks hauling a load of American chairs
into Baja were drenched in a rain of diesel, fired
up with torches: their ribs made smoking cages
to catch your vision, charred hearts
sacrificed to carrion crows.

You couldn't see home on burning days,
the veils of flesh-fired fog cut the sky in half.
You took them clothes on their burning hills,
took them water in white jugs, took
frozen donuts and cans of donated corn.
You went in the name of whatever God you'd cobbled
together from your nightmares and your hopes.
Head lice fell
by the thousands.

This was the dream.

Late, from Mexico, you'd rise
to the neon lightning of America, you'd rise
stinking of dogs and filthy women's armpits, rise

covered in the sweat of men who kill themselves
mining for garbage in coats made of plastic bags.
Bloodmud was caked on your running shoes.
Too tired to run. Undone by days and days
talking to people
with no teeth.

Home, your sweet rock and roll boys, so pretty
with their Bowie hair and their painted girlfriends,
all your best friends so dangerous with their Marlboros,
doing their all-night hang at the donut shop
you peeled a sheet of skin off the back
of a child boiled by overturned cooking pots
of lard
after their gigs at strip bars and bowling alleys.
Coffee and bear claws.

What were you supposed to tell them?
Was Elvis Costello cooler than Joe Jackson?
I saw a human intestine today.
A Gibson SG smokes a Les Paul any day, man,
but a Les Paul is ten times better
than a Strat if you're even going to think about
"Dazed and Confused."
People eating run-over alley dogs.

Ian Dury and the Blockheads buttons
She tried to abort her rape-baby with a wire
On leather jackets.

You didn't even try to sleep.

It was too quiet.

2:00 am.

3:00 am.

Televisions then signed off — showed bleached film
of American flags, static or test patterns:
that Indian chief in the middle looking lost
like you. You had meant to learn to dance.

You, Emperor of Maggots.

That night you knew,
that night it hit you
you were walking
invisible
the abandoned miles of bed-time
Clairemont Drive: duplexes smelling like pot,
your high school already looking small as a fossil.
John Lennon shot in the head.
You'd been holding down a screaming girl
as a doctor peeled scabs off her face
as blood lipsticked her mouth.
Before you found out.

Walking. Clocking.
Quarter mile.
Half mile.
Mile.
Ahead, almost black against the greater black
that man. Facing you,
moving away.
You squinted, sped up: he backed away.
You had to catch up to him — it was all in that
crazy son of a bitch hurrying backward into midnight:
it was all there, in him, and when you got close,
started to say it, he spat at you
backed away running.

You

Stopped.

No moon. No stars. Maybe a Camaro
with glasspaks raced a '68 Mustang to the stoplight.
You had a notebook in your back pocket.
It was too dark to write
What you needed to say:
I have to get away from here.

Biographies

Roger Bonair-Agard is a native of Trinidad and Tobago and a Cave Canem fellow. His first solo collection *tarnish and masquerade* was published this past fall by Cypher Books. He lives in Brooklyn, NY.

Mariah Blackhorse grew up in Chicago suburbs and the front range of the Rocky Mountains. Of mixed Nez Perce and European ancestry, she is also a visual artist and actress, but for her day job she programs computers. Mariah's greatest achievement is being mother to her sons, Dakota and Dylan. She and her family make their home in Bend, Oregon.

Debra Kang Dean's most recent book is *Precipitates* (BOA, 2003). Her poems have appeared in a number of anthologies, including *The Best American Poetry, The New American Poets: A Bread Loaf Anthology*, and *Yobo: Korean American Writing in Hawai'i*. She teaches in the brief-residency MFA in Writing Program at Spalding University and lives in Bloomington, Indiana.

Mitchell L. H. Douglas is an Assistant Professor of Creative Writing at Indiana University-Purdue University Indianapolis (IUPUI) and a member of the creative writing faculty of the Kentucky Governor's School for the Arts. A Cave Canem Fellow and cofounder of the Affrilachian Poets, his poetry appears in *Callaloo* and the anthologies *Poetic Voices Without Borders* (Gival Press) and *The Ringing Ear: Black Poets Lean South* (University of Georgia Press). A native of Louisville, KY, he resides in Indianapolis.

Kelly Norman Ellis is an associate professor of English and creative writing at Chicago State University. She is also the associate director of the MFA in Creative Writing program as CSU. A Cave Canem fellow and founding member of the Affrilachian Poets, her first collection of poetry *Tougaloo Blues* was published by Third World Press in 2003. She lives on Chicago's south side with her partner Kevin and their daughter Naomi Zora.

Yael Flusberg's memoir essays, poetry and reviews have been published in *DC Poets Against the War: An Anthology, Gargoyle, Lilith*, the *Potomac Review, Sojourners,* and *Travelers' Tales*, among others. She works as a coach and consultant with social change organizations, artists, and leaders; is a yoga teacher; and is co-founder of Sol & Soul, a nonprofit which nurtures and promotes emerging and seasoned artists of conscience.

Suheir Hammad a Palestinian-American Brooklyn based poet, artist and activist is the author of *Born Palestinian, Born Black, Drops of This Story* and the recently released *ZaatarDiva*. She has won numerous awards and is the co-writer and original cast member in the Tony-award winning Russell Simmons Presents Def Poetry Jam on Broadway.

Ellen Hagan is a writer, actress and educator. Her poetry has been nominated for a Pushcart Prize and can be seen in *Check the Rhyme: An Anthology of Female Poets & Emcees, and Monologues for Women by Women*. Ellen recently performed for season five of *Russell Simmons Presents Def Poetry Jam* and tours the state with her duo show Becoming Woman. She holds an MFA in fiction from The New School University.

Christine Rose James hails from Louisville, Kentucky, the youngest of three daughters. She was fortunate in having elements of both America and India in her upbringing, an aspect of her life that is reflected in her poetry.

Parneshia Jones is a Chicago writer and a member of the Affrilachian Poets. She has been published in several anthologies including: *Warpland: A Journal of Black Literature and Ideas* and *Limestone*. She has an MFA from Spalding University in Louisville, Kentucky and is currently working on her first poetry collection, *Compasses and Juke Joints*.

Adrian Matejka is a graduate of Southern Illinois University Carbondale. His first collection of poems, *The Devil's Garden*, won the New York/New England Award from Alice James Books.

Tiffany Midge of Hunkpapa Sioux and German ancestry, grew up in the Pacific Northwest. Based in Seattle, she is an enrolled member of the Standing Rock Sioux Reservation. She serves on the Board of Directors for Red Eagle Soaring (RES), the Native American outreach-theater company. She is also a poetry editor for the multicultural arts magazine *The Raven Chronicles. She is the author of Guiding the Stars to Their Campfire, Driving the Salmon to Their Beds*, and *Outlaws, Renegades and Saints : Diary of a Mixed-Up Halfbreed*.

Lee Newton has been twice nominated for a Pushcart Prize. He has received a fellowship from the Illinois Arts Council and a Lannan

Fellowship from the Folger Shakespeare Library. He has won *Amaranth*'s Editor's Choice Award and been a finalist for the Charles Johnson Award in Poetry and the Virginia Down's Poetry Prize. Some of his creative and scholarly works have appeared in the *Wisconsin Review, Crab Orchard Review, Pleiades, Phoebe, Apalachee Review,* and the *Asian Pacific American Journal.* He teaches creative writing, literature, composition, and Business Communication at Bradley University.

Anne Shelby is the author of five children's picture books. A sixth picture book, *The Man Who Lived in a Hollow Tree: An Appalachian Legend* is scheduled for publication in '09. Both of her recently published collections for adults, *Appalachian Studies* (poems) and *Can a Democrat Get Into Heaven? Politics, Religion and Other things You Ain't Suppose to Talk About* (newspaper columns) include selections suitable for young readers. She lives in Clay County, Kentucky, and is an active member of Kentucky Writers Against Mountaintop Removal.

Matthew Shenoda is a Coptic poet whose work has been published widely and supported by the California Arts Council and the Lannan Foundation. A faculty member in the College of Ethnic Studies at San Francisco State University, Shenoda's debut collection of poems, *Somewhere Else* is the winner of a 2006 American Book Award.

Patricia Smith is a four-time national individual champion of the National Poetry Slam. Her latest book, *Teahouse of the Almighty*, was chosen as a 2005 National Poetry Series winner. She is the author of three previous books: *Close to Death, Big Towns, Big Talk* and *Life According to Motown*. Highly anthologized she has also appeared in the feature film *Slamnation* and on *HBO's Def Poetry Jam*.

Bianca Lynne Spriggs is currently an English Instructor at Bowling Green Technical College. An Affrilachian Poet and Cave Canem Fellow, she received her Bachelor's Degree in History at Transylvania University and a Master's Degree in English with an emphasis in Creative Writing at the University of Wisconsin-Milwaukee. She is currently pursuing a second Master's in Folklore at Western Kentucky University.

Frank X Walker is a founding member of the Affrilachian Poets and a Cave Canem Fellow. He is the author of three books of poetry (*Affrilachia, Buffalo Dance: the Journey of York* and *Black Box*) and the publisher and editor of *PLUCK! The Journal of Affrilachian Arts & Culture*. He won a 2005 Lannan Literary Fellowship for Poetry. He currently serves as Visiting Professor of Writing, Rhetoric and Communications at Transylvania University.

Luis Alberto Urrea has published extensively in all the major genres. His first book *Across the Wire*, was named a New York Times Notable Book. He also won a 1999 American Book Award for his memoir, *Nobody's Son: Notes from an American Life*. He was in the *1996 Best American Poetry* collection. He lives with his family in Naperville and teaches creative writing at the University of Illinois at Chicago.

Hao Wang was born in Fuzhou, China. He moved with his family to Kentucky in 1991 — and still considers the Bluegrass a vital part of his identity, despite brief stays in Portland, Oregon, and Philadelphia. A member of the Affrilachian Poets, he currently studies at the University of Pennsylvania — among other things — international business, French, and mathematics.

Kathy Y. Wilson is a Cincinnati based writer and educator. She is the author of the award winning collection of columns, *Your Negro Tour Guide: Truths In Black and White* and contributes regular commentaries to National Public Radio's "All Things Considered." She is also an adjunct Journalism instructor at the University of Cincinnati where she teaches columns and reviews.